Testing and assessment in the National Curriculum

Pupils between the ages of 7 and 11 (Years 3–6) cover Key Stage 2 of the National Curriculum. In May of their final year of Key Stage 2 (Year 6) all pupils take written National Tests (commonly known as SATs) in the three most important subjects: English, Mathematics and Science. Your child may already have taken some National Tests at the end of Key Stage 1 (Year 2). These will have been in number, shape and space, reading, writing, handwriting and spelling.

At the end of Key Stage 1, your child will have been awarded a National Curriculum level for each subject tested. When your child eventually takes the Key Stage 2 tests, he or she again will be awarded a level. On average, pupils are expected to advance one level for every two years they are at school. The target for pupils at the end of Key Stage 1 is Level 2. By the end of Key Stage 2, four years later, the target is Level 4. The table below will show you how your child should progress.

		7 years	11 years
Exceptional performance	Level 6		▓
	Level 5		▒
Exceeded targets for age group	Level 4	▓	░
Achieved targets for age group	Level 3	▒	░
	Level 2	░	░
Working towards targets for age group	Level 1	☐	☐

Assessing your child's progress throughout Key Stage 2 of the National Curriculum

The aim of the Letts Assessment books is to help you monitor your child's progress in English, Mathematics and Science throughout Key Stage 2. There are four books for each subject – one for each year, starting with 7–8 year olds. The questions in the books become progressively harder with each year, so that for 10–11 year olds, the questions will be at a level similar to the Key Stage 2 National Tests.

After completing a book, your child will have a score which you will be able to interpret using the progress indicator provided. This will give you a guide to the level at which your child is working.

ASSESSING YOUR CHILD'S PROGRESS

Using this book to assess your child's progress in English

This book contains four basic features:

Questions: 4 reading tests, based on the English magazine
4 writing tests
1 handwriting test
1 spelling test

Answers: showing acceptable responses and marks

Note to Parent: giving advice on what your child should be doing and how to help

Progress Chart: showing you how to interpret your child's marks to arrive at a level

- The reading tests are based on the magazine at the back, which can be detached. Before starting a reading test, your child should spend some time reading the relevant section of the magazine.

- Your child should not attempt to do all the questions in the book in one go. Try tackling one test at a time or, for the longer reading tests, try ten questions at a time. If your child does not understand the Writing, Handwriting or Spelling Test, you should explain what has to be done. Avoid doing this for the Reading Tests, however – particularly when your child is working on the test. Encourage your child to continue the test and move on to the next question. Afterwards, it is most valuable to go over questions that caused problems.

- When your child has completed the questions, turn to the Answer section at the back of the book. Using the recommended answers, award your child the appropriate mark or marks for each question. In the margin of each question page, there are small boxes. These are divided in half with the marks available for that question at the bottom, and a blank at the top for you to fill in your child's score. Enter the total number of marks at the end of each test.

- Collate your child's marks on the grid on page 34. Then add them up. Once you have the total, turn to page 24 at the front of the Answer section and look at the Progress Chart to determine your child's level.

- Work through the answers with your child, using the Note to Parent to help give advice, correct mistakes and explain problems.

Equipment your child will need for this book

All your child needs are a pen or pencil for writing, and writing paper for the four writing tests (about two sheets for each test). Your child may also like to have a rubber for changing answers.

Instructions

There are four reading tests – one on each section of the magazine:

- On Mother's Day
- Making a Punch and Judy Mask
- Miss Dose the Doctors' Daughter
- The Seaside Man

You can do the reading tests in any order. Take as much time as you wish to read each section of the magazine.

In some questions you will have to put a (ring) round the right answer like this:

Monday is

| a month of the year | the first day of the week |
| a day when all the shops close | **the second day of the week** |

If you find a question difficult, don't worry about it, go on to the next question.

On Mother's Day

Now please read 'On Mother's Day' on page 1 of your magazine. Answer these questions about the poem. You may look at the magazine as often as you wish.

About the poem   **Questions 1–4**

1   What was the **first** thing the children did after they got up?

picked flowers	sang a serenade
started breakfast	wrapped their gifts

1
Q1

2   What did the children hurry to do **after** they picked the flowers?

boil the eggs	make the toast
make coffee	write a card

1
Q2

2

3

What went wrong with the coffee, eggs and toast the children prepared for their mother's breakfast?

3
Q3

a   coffee   ....

b   eggs   ....

c   toast   ....

4

The children made rather a mess of their mother's breakfast but the last line of the poem says "she was smiling to her ears!" Why do you think she was so pleased?

2
Q4

....

....

Total

7
On Mother's Day

Making a Punch and Judy Mask

Now please read 'Making a Punch and Judy Mask' on pages 2–4 of your magazine. Answer these questions about what you have read. You may look at the magazine as often as you wish.

About the instructions   Questions 1–8

1

How many items are needed to make the mask?

1
Q1

2

What kinds of sticking tape are used?

2
Q2

3

What do you use to cut the mask shape out of the cardboard box?

1
Q3

4 You are told to scrunch the newspaper up to make three different features for the face. Name **two** of them.

2
Q4

1... 2...

5 How do you find out how to mix up the wallpaper paste?

1
Q5

....

6 Why is newspaper stuck over the features?

1
Q6

....

7 How is Punch's hat attached to the mask itself?

1
Q7

....

8 Give **two** reasons why the finished mask is covered with a layer of glue?

2
Q8

1..

2..

Letts

Problems that we came across   Questions 9–12

1
Q9

9 Under which part of the face was it difficult to get tape?

....

1
Q10

10 What kept popping up?

the hat   the nose

the newspaper   the white paper

1
Q11

11 What was soggy and wet?

the masking tape   the white paper

the papier mâché   the cheeks

1
Q12

12 Why did Hayleigh find it difficult to design her mask?

....

Your Opinion   Questions 13–15

13

Why do you think the instructions start by telling you the things you will need to make the mask?

✏ ....

....

1
Q13

14

Do you think the mask looks good? Yes/No
Give **two** reasons for your answer.

✏ 1..

✏ 2..

2
Q14

15

If you were making a mask of a police officer, how would you change the design?

✏ ....

....

3
Q15

Total

21

Punch mask

Miss Dose the Doctors' Daughter

Now please read 'Miss Dose the Doctors' Daughter' on pages 5–9 of your magazine and answer these questions about the story. You may look at the magazine as often as you wish.

| About the story | Questions 1–15 |

1   Dora Dose's parents were both

     plumbers   dentists   nurses   doctors

2   In the mornings, Dora tapped her dad's knee with a

     chisel   hammer   finger   spoon

3   In her pretend waiting-room, Dora had six pretend

     bags   chairs   patients   dolls

4   Dora asked those in her waiting-room to say

     "Ah!"   "Ugh!"   "Oh!"   "Hello!"

5 How did Dora feel about her pretend set-up?

happy   excited   unhappy   bored

1
Q5

6 Dora got fed up when her patients

walked silently into the room

asked too many questions

ate all the tablets

wouldn't come into her room

1
Q6

7

What was different about Dora's baby brother when he woke up one morning?

1
Q7

8

Who was the only person not to have spots that morning?

1
Q8

9

What did Dora go and get from her mum and dad's surgery?

1
Q9

10

When did Dora see all the spotty people in her mum and dad's waiting-room?

11

What are **two** things that Dora did to help her parents when they had spots?

1...

2...

12

What did most of the patients say about Dora?

13

When the patients were better, why did they come back to the doctors' house?

14

Why did Dora like being a "real" doctor?

15

What happens to Dora at the end of the story?

1
Q15

....

About the characters   Questions 16–18

16   How would you describe Dora's parents?

1
Q16

They get
cross with Dora for
playing doctors.

They
ignore her.

They join in
her game when she is
playing doctors.

They refuse
to pretend to be
her patients.

17

In your own words, write down **three** things that
show you what kind of person Dora is.

3
Q17

1 ....

2 ....

3 ....

Letts

18

How do you know that Dora has two brothers?

Q18

....

How the story is written   Questions 19–22

19

At the beginning of the story the writer says that Dora is a "double doctor's daughter". What does he mean by this?

Q19

....

....

20 a

What are the first **three** things that Dora does when she goes down to the surgery to look after the spotty patients?

Q20a

 1...

 2...

3...

b What does this tell you about how she feels about her new job?

2

Q20b

....

....

21 Why did Dora feel happy that her real patients never said it was their turn to be the doctor?

1

Q21

....

....

22 At the end of the story, we are told that Dora had a **perfect** patient.

a Who was the perfect patient?

1

Q22a

....

b Why does the writer suggest that this patient would be perfect?

2

Q22b

....

....

13

Your opinion   Questions 23–24

23 What kind of story would you describe this as?

adventure   funny   mystery   sad

24 a What did you like or dislike about this story?

....

....

b Why?

....

....

1
Q23

1
Q24a

2
Q24b

Total
36
Miss Dose

Letts

14

The Seaside Man

Now please read 'The Seaside Man' on pages 10–11 of your magazine and answer these questions about the poem. You may look at the magazine as often as you wish.

About the seaside man	Questions 1–2

1 a

How is the seaside man's left eye described?

1
Q1a

b

How is his right arm described?

1
Q1b

2 Run, run as fast as you can,
I'll catch you 'cos I'm the seaside man.

a

What does the chorus of the poem suggest?

1
Q2a

2

Q2b

b Why do you think this is so?

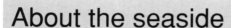

About the seaside   Questions 3–4

3   Waves crash in the rocks on the sandy sea shore,
     Money chinking in the amusements,
     The whistling of the wind,
     The fog horn of a boat,
     The screech of a roller coaster's brakes.

4

Q3

Find **four** words from this verse which describe **sounds** of the seaside and write them here.

1...   2...

3...   4...

4   Parts of the seaside man's body are compared with things you would find at the seaside.

a Write **three** comparisons from the poem.

1 ....

2 ....

3 ....

b Do you like or dislike the comparisons? Why?

1 ....

2 ....

3 ....

Your opinion   Question 5

5 Did you enjoy this poem? Yes/No
Why?

....

....

Letts

Instructions

Ask your parent to read the notes on page 28 before you begin. You can do the writing tests in any order you choose but you should try to do all four.

Spend about ten minutes planning your writing and no longer than an hour doing each test. Ask your parent for some writing paper. When you have finished your writing, check these details:

- spelling and punctuation;
- whether you could have described characters or information in more detail;
- whether you could have written a better beginning or ending.

A Surprise Parcel

1

18
Q1

> Write a short story called 'A Surprise Parcel'.

When planning your story, think about:
- who is the parcel for? (it could be you!)
- what is the surprise?
- does anyone share the surprise?
- what happens as a result of the surprise?

A Magician's Mask

2   A magician has a special mask. Once you put it on, you can become anyone you wish and do anything you like. The magician says you may use the mask for a day.

| Write the story of what happens. |

18

Q2

You may like to include details about:
- how you came to meet the magician;
- how you learnt about the mask;
- who you become for a day;
- what it is like being that person;
- what you choose to do;
- the people you met;
- the adventures you had;
- how the story ends.

Making a Den

3

In 'Making a Punch and Judy Mask' you were given instructions about how to make a mask. Draw up a set of instructions so that you and a friend can make a secret hideaway or den.

Things that you might include in your writing:
- where the den will be built;
- what materials will be needed;
- how to build the den;
- how to make sure that the den is safe;
- how the den will be used.

Taking Alie to School

4

Alie the Alien has landed in a spacecraft near your home. Alie wants to come to school with you. Write to Alie and give instructions about how best to get ready for school.

You will need to think about:
- the things you do to get ready;
- the clothes you wear for school and how you put them on;
- the food you have for breakfast or take to school;
- the things you take to school.

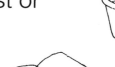

Handwriting test

Here is a short passage for you to copy out in your best handwriting. You may practise this passage as many times as you wish. When doing this handwriting test you should check that:

- you are forming all the letters correctly;
- your letters are the right size;
- you are joining your writing correctly.

Copy this passage:

A month ago,
Old Mr Noah
Had a good idea.
"Oh come aboard," he called,
"And make a home here!"

Write the passage below.

Total

4

Handwriting

Spelling test

Ask your parent to read out the story on page 33. The same story is written below, but it has some words missing. You should follow the story as your parent reads it the first time.

Now your parent will read the story again. When you come to a blank line, wait for your mum or dad to tell you the missing word. Write the word on the line. If you are not sure how to spell it, just try to write the letters you think are correct.

Duncan wanted to be a good footballer, but every time he went to play with the other

.... from his street they would never let him kick the .... Today .... been different. They let him .... in the game and he scored his .... goal. He felt .... as he got ready for bed. Maybe he could be a .... after all! His .... came to tuck him in and turn out the .... Duncan had hardly put his head on the .... and gone to .... before he began to dream.

1
Q1

1
Q2

1
Q3

1
Q4

1
Q5

1
Q6

1
Q7

1
Q8

1
Q9

1
Q10

1
Q11

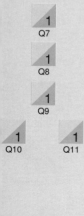

22

He was .... in the World Cup Semi-finals.
His .... needed to .... Brazil to reach the
Final.

Suddenly, he was .... down the wing with
the ball. The Brazilian fullback had stuck close to
Duncan. This player was the .... he had
ever played against and he was getting ....

Duncan kept .... He hoped that he
wouldn't .... up before he reached the
Brazilian penalty area.

Suddenly, there was a big .... and Duncan
woke up to find himself on
the floor!

1
Q12

1   1
Q13   Q14

1
Q15

1
Q16

1
Q17

1
Q18

1
Q19

1
Q20

Total

20
Spelling

23

- When marking your child's questions, remember that the answers given here are the answers the question-setter expects. You must look at your child's answers and judge whether they deserve credit.

- When you go through the questions with your child, try to be positive. Look for good things that have been done as well as discussing where errors have been made. When discussing your child's writing it is valuable to help your child re-draft what he or she has written but remember that re-drafting is mostly about improving the **structure** of the story and not just *"writing it out in best"*.

- Enter your child's marks on the grid on page 34, and then calculate your child's overall score. The table below will help you interpret your child's level for English.

Progress Chart

Total marks scored	Progress made	Suggested action
40 or below	Your child's mark shows that he or she is starting to develop some skills in reading and writing associated with Level 2.	In reading, help your child to identify the main points of passages/books he or she reads. In writing, help your child to think about how to start a story and plan what will happen next.
41–80	A mark in this range indicates that your child is working within Level 2 in both reading and writing.	In reading, help your child to express opinions more fully. Help your child to use more interesting words in his or her writing. Discuss how he or she could include more than two events or statements.
81–101	Your child is consolidating his or her skills in reading and writing at Level 2.	In reading, help your child to express opinions more fully. Use the Writing Marking Keys on pages 29–30 to identify your child's specific needs.
102–131	A mark in this range indicates that your child is working within Level 3.	In reading, help your child to express preferences more fully. In writing, use the Marking Keys to identify your child's specific needs in terms of structuring writing and using more interesting vocabulary.
132 and above	Your child is consolidating his or her skills in reading and writing at Level 3.	In reading, encourage your child to read a wide range of texts. Help him or her to infer meaning from texts and to develop writing by using more complex sentence structures.

- A child at the end of Year 3 (7–8 year olds) should be, of the above statements, between the third and the fourth statements.

Poetry: 'On Mother's Day'

1	started breakfast	*1 mark*
2	make coffee	*1 mark*
3	a the coffee was rather black	*1 mark*
	b the eggs were a little hard	*1 mark*
	c the toast was burned	*1 mark*
4	their mother was happy	

Award 1 mark for the answer; 2 marks for elaboration,
e.g. "she was happy because she knew they had tried hard to please her"   *2 marks*

Total: 7 marks

Note to parent

This was a straightforward test requiring your child to show an ability to accurately locate and identify information from the poem. If your child found this test difficult, you should consider whether he or she should continue working on these reading tests as they become progressively difficult. Children who are working at Level 1 and the early stages of Level 2 often find it difficult to respond in writing to questions about their reading.

Information Writing: 'Making a Punch and Judy Mask'

1	14	*1 mark*
2	double-sided sticky tape	*1 mark*
	masking tape	*1 mark*
3	scissors	*1 mark*
4	• nose	
	• cheeks	
	• forehead	
	Any two answers: 1 mark each	*2 marks*
5	You read the instructions on the packet	*1 mark*
6	Accept any answer which refers to securing the features in place	*1 mark*
7	by using double-sided sticky tape	*1 mark*
8	to make the mask shiny	*1 mark*
	to make the mask strong/tough	*1 mark*
9	the nose	*1 mark*
10	the newspaper	*1 mark*
11	the papier mâché	*1 mark*
12	She had never seen a Punch and Judy show in her life	*1 mark*
13	Credit any response that indicates that it is best if people are told the materials they will need before starting to make the mask	*1 mark*
14	No credit for Yes/No response. Reasons should be more than "I like it" but "I liked it because it is funny" is sufficient	
	Any two reasons: 1 mark each	*2 marks*
15	Changes in design might include different:	
	• features (not such a big nose)	
	• hat (cap or helmet)	
	• facial expression	
	Any three changes: 1 mark each	*3 marks*

Total: 21 marks

Narrative Writing: 'Miss Dose the Doctors' Daughter'

1 doctors — *1 mark*
2 hammer — *1 mark*
3 patients — *1 mark*
4 "Ah!" — *1 mark*
5 unhappy — *1 mark*
6 wouldn't come into her room — *1 mark*
7 he was covered in spots — *1 mark*
8 Dora — *1 mark*
9 the spots medicine — *1 mark*
10 nine o'clock in the morning (accept nine o'clock or morning) — *1 mark*
11 got them the spots medicine — *1 mark*
she saw their patients — *1 mark*
12 They said Dora was a *little* doctor — *1 mark*
13 The patients came back to thank Dora — *1 mark*
14 Accept reasons such as:
• she took the job seriously
• the patients did not want to take turns at being the doctor
Any two reasons: 1 mark each — *2 marks*
15 She is covered in spots — *1 mark*
16 They join in her game when she is playing doctors. — *1 mark*
17 • Dora is helpful/sensible/kind
• she gets fed up when people don't go along with her game
• she likes to play pretend games/doctors
• she is serious about the games she plays
Any three responses: 1 mark each — *3 marks*
18 The writer says that Dora has a *little* brother and a *baby* brother — *1 mark*
19 He means that both her parents are doctors — *1 mark*
20 a • she puts on her mum's white coat
• picks up her dad's stethoscope
• sits down in the doctor's chair
Three actions: 1 mark each — *3 marks*
b • she takes the job seriously
• she wants to do well
Any two reasons: 1 mark each — *2 marks*

21		It meant that she could be the doctor all the time/without argument	*1 mark*
22	a	Dora	*1 mark*
	b	Answers should reflect that because Dora knew how she wanted her patients to behave she would know how to be a perfect patient	*2 marks*
23		funny	*1 mark*
24	a	Accept any response that indicates like or dislike	*1 mark*
	b	Accept any reason which explains "like" or "dislike", for example, "I didn't like the story as I thought Dora was silly." *Any two reasons: 1 mark each*	*2 marks*

Total: 36 marks

Note to parent

The questions at the beginning of each section ask your child to identify the main elements of the story. Many of the harder questions ask for opinions or reasons for a particular response. Children working at Level 2 in Reading should be able to identify the main elements of a story and offer an opinion. At Level 3 they are expected to express preferences and opinions about what they read.

Some children find difficulty in answering questions where they have to give reasons or opinions. If you notice this, help your child to answer the questions orally. Once he or she can "say" the answer, help your child to "write" it.

Poetry: 'The Seaside Man'

1	a	a stinging jellyfish	*1 mark*
	b	Blackpool Tower	*1 mark*
2	a	that no matter how fast you run the seaside man will catch you	*1 mark*
	b	Answers might reflect that the seaside man: • moves very quickly • is huge • can move in any direction quickly • is very powerful or strong *Any two answers: 1 mark each*	*2 marks*
3		crash	*1 mark*
		chinking	*1 mark*
		whistling	*1 mark*
		screech	*1 mark*
4	a	*Any three comparisons from the poem: 1 mark each*	*3 marks*
	b	Reasons should explain why a comparison is liked or disliked *Any three reasons: 1 mark each*	*3 marks*
5		No mark for Yes/No response – the answer must **explain** the Yes or No response.	*1 mark*

Total: 16 marks

Note to parent

The questions on this poem are quite challenging and many children find it more difficult to respond to poetry. Your child was asked to give reasons and explain preferences in many of the questions. There were also questions about the words and description used in the poem. If your child has found it difficult to respond to these types of question you may wish to go through them and help your child to answer them orally.

Notes for parents on the writing tests

The National Curriculum places importance on children having a range of writing experiences. Your child should try all four tests but they can be tried in any order.

Each starting point suggests ideas or information that your child might wish to include in his or her writing. Before your child begins, he or she should spend a little time planning (about ten minutes). You may wish to help with this. By helping your child to plan the organisation of his or her writing, you will help him or her to develop writing skills. The marking keys can also guide you to help your child with his or her writing, by showing how writing skills should develop between two levels.

Make sure your child has about two sheets of writing paper for each test. Your child should spend no longer than one hour doing each test.

Marking keys

Use the marking keys on pages 29–30 to make a decision about your child's writing level in each piece of writing. Use the first key to mark 'A Surprise Parcel' and 'A Magician's Mask'; use the second key to mark 'Making a Den' and 'Taking Alie to School'. Turn to page 31 to find out how to award marks using each key.

Marking key – stories

How is the story written and organised?	Q1 Yes No	Q2 Yes No
LEVEL 2		
Does the story have an opening? (e.g. "One day...")	☐ ☐	☐ ☐
Is there more than one character/person?	☐ ☐	☐ ☐
Are there at least two events which follow each other?	☐ ☐	☐ ☐
Is the writing like ordinary speech? (e.g. "I am having a good time")	☐ ☐	☐ ☐
Are simple sentences used (or sentences joined by "and')?	☐ ☐	☐ ☐
Are some interesting words used (e.g. "lovely" instead of "nice") ?	☐ ☐	☐ ☐
LEVEL 3		
Does the story relate to the title?	☐ ☐	☐ ☐
Are there some interesting details? (suspense, humour, description)	☐ ☐	☐ ☐
Are the thoughts or feelings of the characters described?	☐ ☐	☐ ☐
Are there several connected events that follow each other?	☐ ☐	☐ ☐
Does the story feel as though it has been written with a reader in mind?	☐ ☐	☐ ☐
Does the story have a simple ending?	☐ ☐	☐ ☐
Are descriptive phrases used? (e.g. "a sunny day")	☐ ☐	☐ ☐
Are joining words such as "but" or "because" used?	☐ ☐	☐ ☐
Are adverbs used? (e.g. "quickly", "slowly")	☐ ☐	☐ ☐

How is the story presented?	Q1 Yes No	Q2 Yes No
LEVEL 2		
Are capital letters and full stops used correctly in one or two places?	☐ ☐	☐ ☐
Are most of the simple words (good/help/shop) spelt correctly?	☐ ☐	☐ ☐
Are most of the letters of similar size (a,c,o) formed correctly?	☐ ☐	☐ ☐
LEVEL 3		
Are capital letters and full stops used correctly in half the sentences?	☐ ☐	☐ ☐
Are most of the common longer words spelt correctly (family, together)?	☐ ☐	☐ ☐
Is the handwriting legible with some letters joined up?	☐ ☐	☐ ☐

Marking key – information writing

How is the information written and organised?	Q3 Yes No	Q4 Yes No
LEVEL 2		
Does the writing have some simple structure?	☐ ☐	☐ ☐
Does the writing include a number of statements?	☐ ☐	☐ ☐
Does the writing contain some simple information?	☐ ☐	☐ ☐
Is the writing like ordinary speech?	☐ ☐	☐ ☐
Are simple sentences used (or sentences joined by "and")?	☐ ☐	☐ ☐
Are some interesting words used? (e.g. "lovely" instead of "nice")	☐ ☐	☐ ☐
LEVEL 3		
Does the writing have a simple introduction?	☐ ☐	☐ ☐
Does the writing include a number of linked statements?	☐ ☐	☐ ☐
Does the writing contain information described in some detail to add interest?	☐ ☐	☐ ☐
Does the writing have a simple ending?	☐ ☐	☐ ☐
Does the writing show an awareness of the intended reader? (e.g. Alie or a friend)	☐ ☐	☐ ☐
Are descriptive phrases used? (e.g. "a snug den")	☐ ☐	☐ ☐
Are joining words such as "but" or "because" used?	☐ ☐	☐ ☐
Are adverbs used? (e.g. "quickly", "slowly")	☐ ☐	☐ ☐

How is the information presented?	Q3 Yes No	Q4 Yes No
LEVEL 2		
Are capital letters and full stops used correctly in one or two places?	☐ ☐	☐ ☐
Are most of the simple words (good/help/shop) spelt correctly?	☐ ☐	☐ ☐
Are most of the letters of similar size (a,c,o) formed correctly?	☐ ☐	☐ ☐
LEVEL 3		
Are capital letters and full stops used correctly in half the sentences?	☐ ☐	☐ ☐
Are most of the common longer words spelt correctly (family, together)?	☐ ☐	☐ ☐
Is the handwriting legible with some letters joined up?	☐ ☐	☐ ☐

Deciding the level of attainment:

For each piece of writing, follow the steps below.

Using the keys provided, decide which level best describes your child's writing in a particular test. Award marks from the range given according to how well you feel your child's writing meets the criteria. Fill in the marks on the marking grid on page 34.

1   Start with the questions for Level 2.

- If you are only able to respond yes to a small number of questions then your child is working at the early stages of Level 2. Where you are answering yes to only one or two of the questions then your child is probably at an earlier stage of development and working at Level 1;

(award up to 4 marks)

- If you are able to answer yes to most or all of the questions, your child's work is well within the area of Level 2 writing and you should go on to consider the Level 3 questions. If you are unable to award marks using Level 3 questions, award 6 marks;

(award 6 marks)

2   Using the Level 3 questions:

- where you are able to answer yes to only one or two questions your child is working mainly in the area of Level 2;

(award 7–10 marks)

- where you are able to answer yes to about half the questions your child is starting to move on from Level 2 and is working towards Level 3;

(award 11–14 marks)

- where you are able to answer yes to most or all of the questions your child is working well within Level 3 and you may wish to consider providing work to help development at Level 4, particularly if this is his or her attainment on all the writing tests.

(award 15–18 marks)

A parent's guide to the handwriting test

The handwriting test consists of one passage that your child should copy out in his or her best handwriting. The test focuses mainly on two groups of letters:

- c, o, a, g, d, e;
- r, n, m, h.

Your child may practise the test or words from it as often as is helpful. The emphasis of the test is on:

- correct letter formation;
- correct size;
- starting to join letters correctly.

The handwriting test should be scored as follows:

The letters c, o, a, g, d are formed correctly.
The letters "start at the side"
e.g. .... *cag* .... or ...... *c a* ....
in a cursive style. Both are formed in **one**
continuous movement **not two** e.g. ...... *a d* ......   *1 mark*

The letters r, n, m, h are all formed correctly.
The letters go "down and round"
e.g. .... *r n m* .... or ...... *r n m* ....
in a cursive style. Both are formed in **one** continuous
movement **not two** e.g. ...... *r h* ......   *1 mark*

The letters c, a, o, r, n, m, i, e all should be a
similar size and be about half the height of the
line used.   *1 mark*

The passage is written in a legible joined style.   *1 mark*

Total: 4 marks

A parent's guide to the spelling test

Your child's version of the spelling test is printed on pages 22–23. This test consists of a short story with blank spaces which have to be filled with the spelling test words. The story is written out in full for you below and you can detach it if you wish.

Read the text of the story out loud to your child **twice**. The first time read it through without stopping so that your child gets the sense of the story. Then read it a second time, pausing where your child has to write in the missing words in his or her version of the story.

In your text, the words printed in bold italics are the words your child will have to spell.

Spelling test – for parents to read aloud

Duncan wanted to be a good footballer, but every time he went to play with the other *children* from his street they would never let him kick the *ball*. Today *had* been different. They let him *play* in the game and he scored his *first* goal. He felt *good* as he got ready for bed. Maybe he could be a *star* after all! His *mother* came to tuck him in and turn out the *light*. Duncan had hardly put his head on the *pillow* and gone to *sleep* before he began to dream.

He was *playing* in the World Cup Semi-finals. His *team* needed to *beat* Brazil to reach the Final.

Suddenly, he was *running* down the wing with the ball. The Brazilian fullback had stuck close to Duncan. This player was the *fastest* he had ever played against and he was getting *closer*.

Duncan kept *going*. He hoped that he wouldn't *wake* up before he reached the Brazilian penalty area.

Suddenly, there was a big *crash* and Duncan woke up to find himself on the floor!

Spelling test answers – parent's marking guide

1	children	**6**	good	**11**	sleep	**16**	fastest
2	ball	**7**	star	**12**	playing	**17**	closer
3	had	**8**	mother	**13**	team	**18**	going
4	play	**9**	light	**14**	beat	**19**	wake
5	first	**10**	pillow	**15**	running	**20**	crash

The score from the spelling test is converted into marks which contribute to the overall level for writing. Marks should be given as follows:

Number of correct words	Marks
0–5	1
6–10	2
11–15	3
16–20	4

Note to parent

The marks from this test should be transferred to the marking grid overleaf.

MARKING GRID

READING **Pages 2–17**

Test	Marks available	Marks scored
'On Mother's Day'	7	
'Making a Punch and Judy Mask'	21	
'Miss Dose the Doctors' Daughter'	36	
'The Seaside Man'	16	
Total	**80**	

WRITING **Pages 18–23**

Test	Marks available	Marks scored
A Surprise Parcel	18	
A Magician's Mask	18	
Making a Den	18	
Taking Alie to School	18	
Handwriting (see page 32)	**4**	
Spelling (see overleaf)	**4**	
Total	**80**	

TO CALCULATE AN OVERALL ENGLISH SCORE

Before calculating an overall score for English, work out your child's level of attainment in Reading and Writing separately. Determining these levels separately will allow you to identify your child's particular strengths and weaknesses in English. Record your child's scores in each test in the grids provided.

Determining a level for Reading

Below Level 2	Level 2	Level 3
0–18	19–49	50–80

Determining a level for Writing

Below Level 2	Level 2	Level 3
0–21	22–51	52–80

When all the tests have been completed you will be able to work out the overall total for English.

Totals	Marks available	Marks scored
Reading total	80	
Writing total	80	
Total for English	**160**	

Use the progress chart on page 24 to determine your child's overall level in English. The chart also suggests ways for you to help improve your child's reading and writing.

On Mother's Day

On Mother's Day we got up first,
so full of plans we almost burst.

We started breakfast right away
as our surprise for Mother's Day.

We picked some flowers, then hurried back
to make the coffee – rather black.

We wrapped our gifts and wrote a card
and boiled the eggs – a little hard.

And then we sang a serenade,
which burned the toast, I am afraid.

But Mother said, amidst our cheers,
"Oh, what a big surprise, my dears.
I've not had such a treat in years."
And she was smiling to her ears!

by Aileen Fisher

Making a Punch and Judy Mask

Lots of children like to make things, at home and at school. Here are some instructions to make a mask. One girl who tried it writes about what happened. Read these instructions – see if you understand them!

You will need:

- a cardboard box
- white paper strips
- glue
- wallpaper paste
- paints
- scissors
- paintbrush
- newspaper strips
- masking tape
- double-sided sticky tape
- water
- card
- craft knife
- plastic bowl

Instructions:

1 Cut out the corner of a cardboard box using scissors, as shown in the picture.

2 Using a craft knife, cut out holes for the eyes and for the mouth.

3 Next make the features of the face. Carefully scrunch up newspaper into a long nose shape and secure to the box using masking tape. Do the same for the cheeks. Build up a forehead above the eyes in the same way.

4 In a plastic bowl, mix the wallpaper paste with the water as instructed on the packet.

5 Dip the strips of newspaper into the paste and stick onto the mask, until the entire face is covered and the features are secure.

6 Leave mask to dry until there are no damp patches left.

7 Repeat step five, but this time use strips of plain white paper.

8 Repeat step six.

9 Paint your mask carefully, highlighting the various features: nose, cheeks, chin, eyes. Leave the paint to dry thoroughly.

10 Cut out the shape for Punch's hat using card, as shown in the picture.

11 Decorate the hat in your own design, using paint. Leave to dry.

12 Attach double-sided sticky tape to the bottom inside edge of the hat, and stick the hat to Punch's forehead.

13 Using a paintbrush, cover the entire mask with a layer of glue. This will make the mask shiny and tough. Leave to dry.

Now the mask is finished.

Hayleigh, age eight, writes about the problems she had when she made a mask.

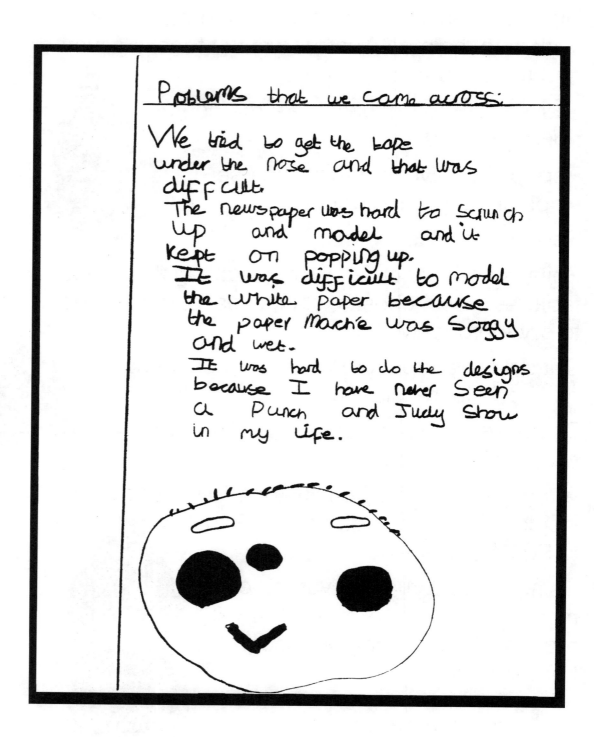

Problems that we came across:

We tried to get the tape under the nose and that was difficult.
The newspaper was hard to scrunch up and model and it kept on popping up.
It was difficult to model the white paper because the paper mâché was soggy and wet.
It was hard to do the designs because I have never seen a Punch and Judy show in my life.

Miss Dose the Doctors' Daughter

Written by Allan Ahlberg, with pictures by Faith Jaques

Dora Dose was a doctor's daughter. Well, really she was a double doctor's daughter. Her mum was a doctor and her dad was a doctor. Dora liked to pretend <u>she</u> was a doctor.

Each morning, when her dad came down to breakfast, he said, "Is there a doctor in the house?" And Dora shouted, "Yes – me!" She took his temperature and tapped his knee with her little doctor's hammer. She told him to say "Ah!"

Dora Dose had a pretend doctor's bag, a pretend doctor's waiting-room and six pretend patients.

Dora's patients were: her little brother, her baby brother, her teddy, two dolls and – sometimes – the cat.

Dora took their temperatures and tapped their knees with her little doctor's hammer. She told them to say "Ah!"

But Dora was not happy being a pretend doctor. Her thermometer didn't really work. Her doctor's hammer was a toy. Her patients would not do as they were told.

"Next please!" said Dora. And her little brother said, "It's <u>my</u> turn to be the doctor." "Next please!" said Dora. And her baby brother crawled off.

"Next please!" said Dora. And the cat <u>ran</u> off. "Next please!" said Dora. And the teddy and the dolls ... just sat there.

"I wish I was a real doctor," said Dora. And she went into the kitchen and bandaged up her mum. Then – one morning – this happened. Dora Dose woke up and went into her baby brother's room.

She was thinking of taking his temperature. But what did she find? Her baby brother was awake, smiling – and <u>covered in spots</u>!

"Oh!" said Dora. She ran into her little brother's room. He was covered in spots, too.

Then she ran into her parents' room, and they were covered in spots. "Is there a doctor in the house?" said Mr Dose. And Dora said, "Yes – me!" "What we need is the spots medicine," said Mrs Dose. She began to get out of bed. "I'll go," said Dora.

Dora went downstairs to her mum and dad's surgery. She got the spots medicine. She gave her dad a spoonful, her mum a spoonful, her little brother a spoonful . She also tapped her baby brother's knee and told him to say "Ah!"

At nine o'clock Dora looked in her mum and dad's waiting-room And what did she find? Lots of patients waiting – <u>real</u> patients – real <u>spotty</u> patients!

"What they need is the spots medicine," said Mr Dose. He began to get out of bed. "I'll go," said Dora.

Dora went downstairs to the surgery again. She put on her mum's white coat. She picked up her dad's stethoscope. She sat in the doctor's chair.

"Next please!" said Dora. And the first patient came in. "You're a little doctor," he said. "Yes," said Dora. She gave him a bottle of spots medicine.

"Next please!" said Dora. And the second patient came in. "You're a <u>very</u> little doctor," she said. "Yes," said Dora. She gave her <u>two</u> bottles.

"Next please!" said Dora. And the next patient came in – and the next – and the next – and the next. Most of them said what a little doctor Dora was. None of them said it was <u>their</u> turn to be the doctor.

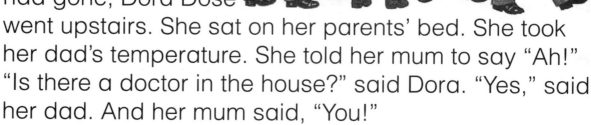

When all the patients had gone, Dora Dose went upstairs. She sat on her parents' bed. She took her dad's temperature. She told her mum to say "Ah!" "Is there a doctor in the house?" said Dora. "Yes," said her dad. And her mum said, "You!"

A few days later, the doorbell rang at the doctors' house. Mr Dose opened the door. And what did he find? It was all those patients again. They had come to say "thank you". Their spots had gone. "Is there a <u>little</u> doctor in the house?" they said. "Well," said Mr Dose, "there's a little <u>spotty</u> doctor."

And so there was. Doctor Dora was up in her room, as happy as could be. She had a real doctor's bag, a real thermometer, a real hammer...

Say "Ah!"

Ah!

... and a perfect patient.

The End

A primary school class wrote this poem together. Try to imagine what the seaside man is like.

Seaside Man

Run, run as fast as you can,
I'll catch you 'cos I'm the seaside man.

His head is a beach ball,
A red octopus is his hair,
His mouth is a pair of swimming trunks,
Each ear is a giant crab,
His right eye is a speckled stone,
A stinging jellyfish is his left eye,
His nose is the head of a swordfish.

Run, run as fast as you can,
I'll catch you 'cos I'm the seaside man.

Waves crash in the rocks on the sandy sea shore,
Money chinking in the amusements,
The whistling of the wind,
The fog horn of a boat,
The screech of a roller coaster's brakes.

Run, run as fast as you can,
I'll catch you 'cos I'm the seaside man.

His body is a roller coaster,
Blackpool Tower is his right arm,
His left arm is a giant slide,
His fingers are MASSIVE lollipop sticks,
Masses of seaweed are his toes,
His right leg is the sea wall,
A sunken galleon's mast is his left leg.

Run, run as fast as you can,
I'll catch you 'cos I'm the seaside man
BIG AND BAD.
GET RUNNING READER!

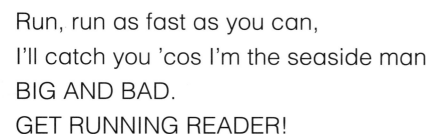